Life's Jungle

Written & Illustrated by:
S. Finelli

AuthorHouse™
1663 Liberty Drive
Bloomington, IN 47403
www.authorhouse.com
Phone: 833-262-8899

Because of the dynamic nature of the Internet, any web addresses or links contained in this book may have changed
since publication and may no longer be valid. The views expressed in this work are solely those of the author and do not
necessarily reflect the views of the publisher, and the publisher hereby disclaims any responsibility for them.

Any people depicted in stock imagery provided by Getty Images are models,
and such images are being used for illustrative purposes only.
Certain stock imagery © Getty Images.

This book is printed on acid-free paper.

ISBN: 978-1-6655-1522-1 (sc)
ISBN: 978-1-6655-1523-8 (e)

Library of Congress Control Number: 2021901521

Print information available on the last page.

Published by AuthorHouse 02/17/2021

authorHOUSE®

This book is dedicated to my *wild* and *wonderful* Ya Ya sisters.

Jungles are known as the lungs of the planet. Along with rainforests, their thick vegetation and trees store vast amounts of carbon dioxide and convert it into life-sustaining oxygen. While jungles have floors dense with tangled vines and shrubs, rainforests have canopies of taller trees that block out much of the sunlight from reaching the ground. Both are found in regions throughout the world and support a diversity of plants, animals, and insects. As with all life on earth, there is interconnectedness between all that exists. Everything depends on other organisms to survive. This reliance extends to abiotic aspects of an ecosystem, such as the decomposing of matter. Understanding this incredible flow of energy within these habitats can help you appreciate your connection with others and the world in which you live.

Lion

'King of the Jungle' is the honor given to the African lion whose roar can be heard for up to five miles away. While this magnificent creature is seen in the jungle, it most often inhabits grasslands and savannas. Lions live in groups, called prides, of up to thirty cats. The lionesses are the primary hunters that use intelligent tactics such as a team approach to capture their prey. It is the male that touts the prominent mane ~ a symbol of its fighting ability. In addition to a lion's running speed of up to 50mph, it can easily climb the trunks of trees. A lion will spend most of the daytime sleeping or lying around to conserve energy then become more active at night. The lion is significant to a terrestrial ecosystem such as the tropical rainforest. It keeps the population of large mammal herbivores under control. If unregulated, herds of elephants, giraffes, zebras, and hippos would significantly reduce vegetation and other species' food sources.

The lion shows you how to be the king, or queen, of your life. Have the courage to walk your own path with integrity. Embrace the magnificence of being YOU! Your presence's strength is capable of balancing the energy dynamics among family, friends, and all those with whom you come in contact.

Orangutan

The orangutan is considered a great ape and the heaviest of tree-dwelling primates. It spends most of its life traveling from tree to tree in a jungle's canopy. An orangutan has an arm span of over seven feet from fingertip to fingertip. It is amazingly dexterous, using both hands and feet to climb, grip tools, gather food, and eat. Young orangutans learn most of what they need to survive from their mothers. They ride on her body, sleep in her nest, and stay with her until the age of seven. With the long learning curve of their young, orangutans give birth once every 7-9 years. An orangutan makes a new sleeping platform every night by weaving together a variety of branches. Orangutans need vast stretches of forests to exist and can live 50 years. These amazing apes provide models for human behavior and the evolution of intelligent species.

The orangutan reminds you of your powerful bond to nature and how it can significantly impact your health. Enjoy time outdoors breathing the fresh air and soaking in the sun. Whether you pitch a tent or take a walk in the park, you will feel more grounded and at peace when you make these kinds of connections to the earth.

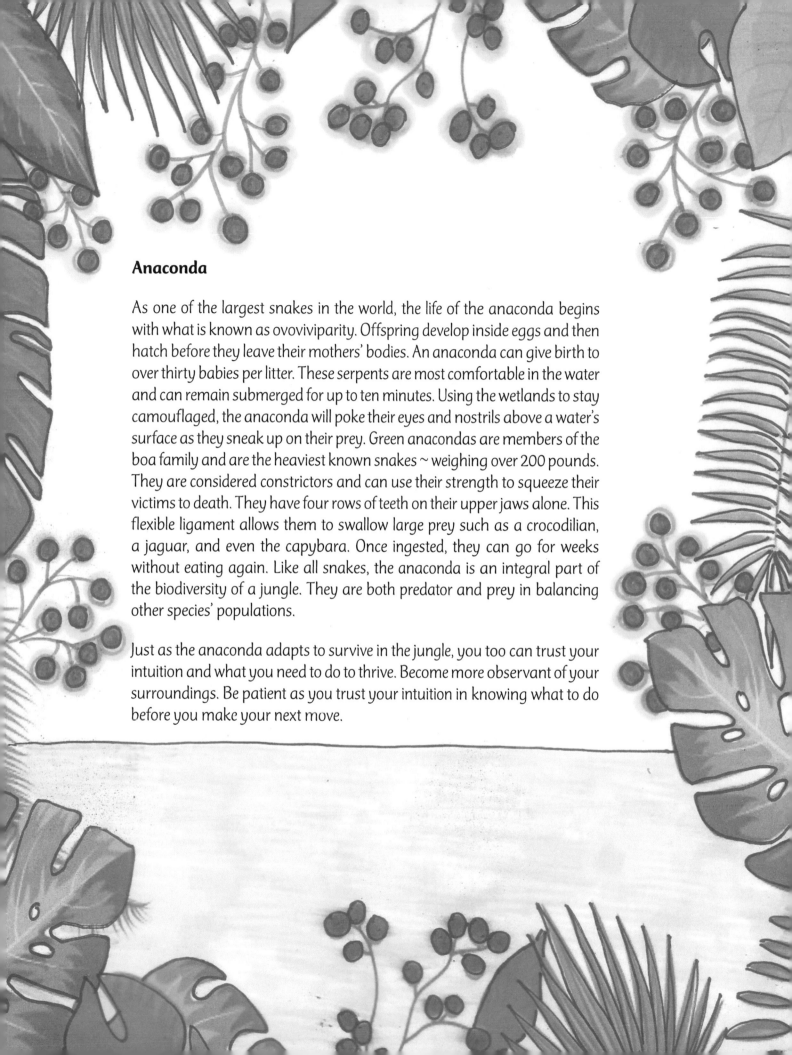

Anaconda

As one of the largest snakes in the world, the life of the anaconda begins with what is known as ovoviviparity. Offspring develop inside eggs and then hatch before they leave their mothers' bodies. An anaconda can give birth to over thirty babies per litter. These serpents are most comfortable in the water and can remain submerged for up to ten minutes. Using the wetlands to stay camouflaged, the anaconda will poke their eyes and nostrils above a water's surface as they sneak up on their prey. Green anacondas are members of the boa family and are the heaviest known snakes ~ weighing over 200 pounds. They are considered constrictors and can use their strength to squeeze their victims to death. They have four rows of teeth on their upper jaws alone. This flexible ligament allows them to swallow large prey such as a crocodilian, a jaguar, and even the capybara. Once ingested, they can go for weeks without eating again. Like all snakes, the anaconda is an integral part of the biodiversity of a jungle. They are both predator and prey in balancing other species' populations.

Just as the anaconda adapts to survive in the jungle, you too can trust your intuition and what you need to do to thrive. Become more observant of your surroundings. Be patient as you trust your intuition in knowing what to do before you make your next move.

Sloths

Sloths are tree-dwelling creatures. They have two to three toes depending on their species and a tongue that extends 10-12 inches out of its mouth for acquiring food. The sloth has a four-part stomach used to break down the tough leaves that they eat. Because of its slow digestion, a sloth has little energy to move about, making it one of the world's most lifeless animals. It moves 6.5 feet per minute on the ground and 10 feet per minute in a tree. The sloth has long, sharp claws that it uses to hold on to branches and defend against predators. This defensive feature is essential when it leaves the tree about once a week to eliminate its bowels. The sloth's interconnectedness to the jungle is significant. Its thick fur and slow movements make it an ideal dwelling for insects, fungi, and algae. In turn, this mutualistic arrangement provides the sloth with green colored camouflage.

The sloth totem requires you to discern between being lazy and relaxing. Much depends on the situation. Laziness in school or the responsibilities of a job is something you want to avoid. However, if you are going through a stressful time, you may need to take more time to relax. Whether you need to be productive, or are experiencing down time, be mindful of every moment.

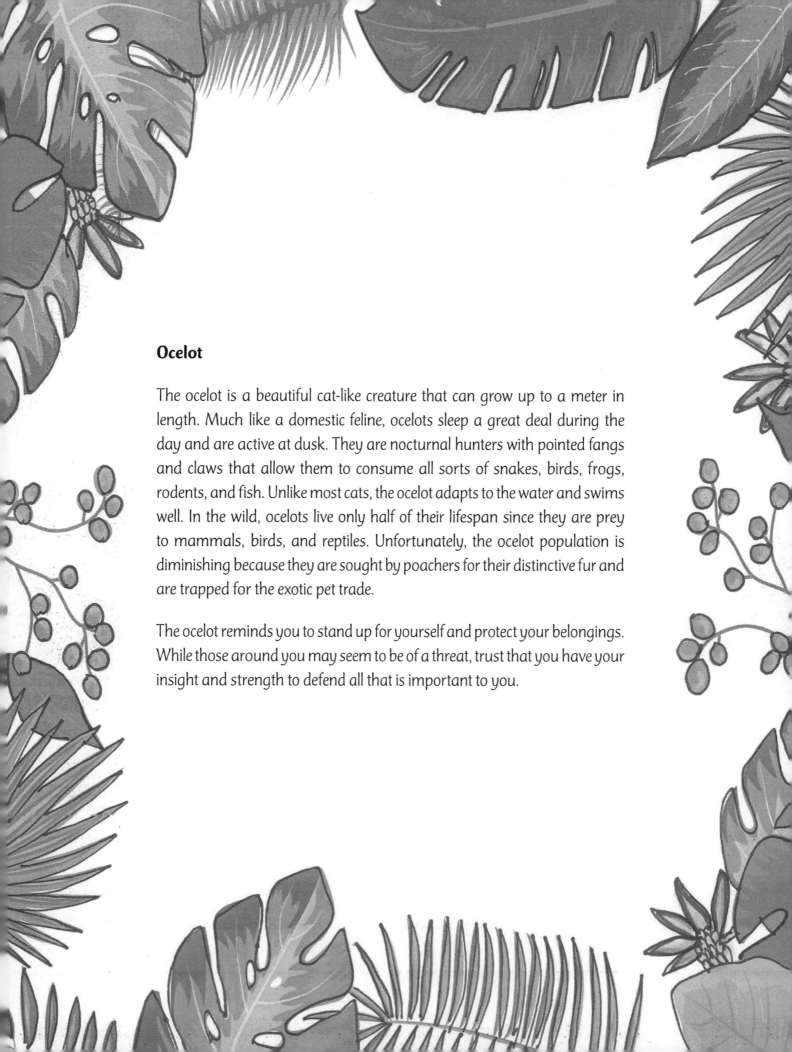

Ocelot

The ocelot is a beautiful cat-like creature that can grow up to a meter in length. Much like a domestic feline, ocelots sleep a great deal during the day and are active at dusk. They are nocturnal hunters with pointed fangs and claws that allow them to consume all sorts of snakes, birds, frogs, rodents, and fish. Unlike most cats, the ocelot adapts to the water and swims well. In the wild, ocelots live only half of their lifespan since they are prey to mammals, birds, and reptiles. Unfortunately, the ocelot population is diminishing because they are sought by poachers for their distinctive fur and are trapped for the exotic pet trade.

The ocelot reminds you to stand up for yourself and protect your belongings. While those around you may seem to be of a threat, trust that you have your insight and strength to defend all that is important to you.

Red-Eyed Frog

Red-eyed tree frogs are easily recognizable. They depict the rare and precious creatures that inhabit the rainforest. For these amphibians, their striking forms are much more practical. The red-eyed tree frog's neon-green bodies, large orange webbed feet, and bulging scarlet eyes act as a detour for predators. Known as 'startle coloration', birds and snakes seeking their next meal may pause when seeing them, which allows for a safe escape. During the day, the red-eyed frog stays out of sight and asleep beneath leaf bottoms. At night, it hides in the canopy and will ambush insects with its long, sticky tongue. Since frogs are amphibians, they are sensitive to the health of both land and water. Therefore, they are a natural bioindicator for the health of the rainforest. Although frogs have been around for millions of years, current environmental stressors have seriously affected their population. They are showing signs of deformities and mutations and are dying off in record numbers.

Just as frogs cannot withstand a toxic environment, you also need to release emotions that can negatively impact your life. The frog essence prompts you to take care of yourself. Be aware of the kind of air you are breathing and the nutrition in the food that you eat. The conditions in which you live can make all the difference in the quality of your health.

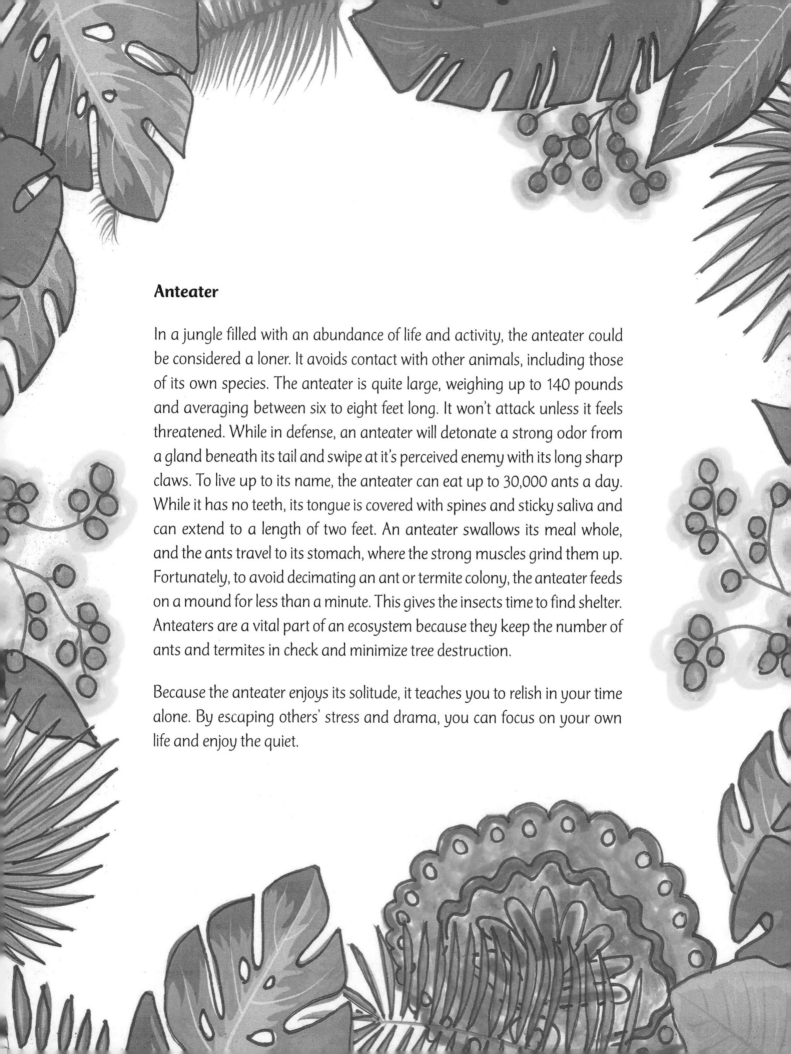

Anteater

In a jungle filled with an abundance of life and activity, the anteater could be considered a loner. It avoids contact with other animals, including those of its own species. The anteater is quite large, weighing up to 140 pounds and averaging between six to eight feet long. It won't attack unless it feels threatened. While in defense, an anteater will detonate a strong odor from a gland beneath its tail and swipe at it's perceived enemy with its long sharp claws. To live up to its name, the anteater can eat up to 30,000 ants a day. While it has no teeth, its tongue is covered with spines and sticky saliva and can extend to a length of two feet. An anteater swallows its meal whole, and the ants travel to its stomach, where the strong muscles grind them up. Fortunately, to avoid decimating an ant or termite colony, the anteater feeds on a mound for less than a minute. This gives the insects time to find shelter. Anteaters are a vital part of an ecosystem because they keep the number of ants and termites in check and minimize tree destruction.

Because the anteater enjoys its solitude, it teaches you to relish in your time alone. By escaping others' stress and drama, you can focus on your own life and enjoy the quiet.

Scarlet Macaw

The macaw is a type of parrot that is easily recognizable by its varied bright colors. The scarlet breed is one of the largest as it can grow to 32 inches. Half of this bird's length consists of a tail, which explains its light weight of only a few pounds. The scarlet macaw uses its powerful white and black bill to break the nuts' shells in their diet and to assist them in climbing. They are able to eat fruits that are poisonous to other jungle creatures. One reason for this immunity is their consumption of clay, which neutralizes plant toxins. In addition to their different types of screams and low-pitched noises used for communication, the scarlet macaw can mimic human speech. This quality could be one reason why they make popular pets. Unfortunately, because of their demand in black markets, their populations are in sharp decline.

The macaw invites you to let your true colors shine. Don't be afraid to show your uniqueness. Be bright, bold, and boisterous as your spirit prompts you.

Tiger

A tiger is the largest of wild cats. A male Royal Bengal can weigh over 660 pounds. One swipe from its massive front hand is enough to kill a person. Tigers are considered nocturnal in that they prefer to hunt at night to avoid human conflict. Tiger cubs are born blind and need to rely on the scent of their mother to survive. Unfortunately, half of the cubs in a liter end up dying of cold or hunger because they cannot keep up. Tigers enjoy being in the water and can swim for hours. According to the World Wildlife Foundation, protecting tigers and their habitat can have unseen benefits to our planet, including the mitigation of climate change, the conservation of freshwater, the preservation of endangered wildlife, and the survival of traditional and indigenous people. When efforts are made to protect the environment for even one species, such as the tiger, it can have far-reaching effects.

A tiger's presence is fearsome. It's spirit cautions you to restrain yourself from acting on aggressive feelings. Have strength when handling intense emotions. Taking time to breathe before you act keeps you from regretting impulsive actions. Your power is best when channeled appropriately.

Capybara

The capybara is actually a rodent ~ the largest on the planet. This creature is semi-aquatic in that it is adapted for life in water as well as the land. The capybara is a strong swimmer, much like a beaver. It has toes that are partially webbed for paddling and long, brittle fur that dries quickly on land. A capybara has an odd diet in that it eats its own feces in the morning when it is rich in protein from the previous day's meal. The capybara can live in groups of up to forty but can easily survive on its own. The capybara's activity depends on its many predators and must remain vigilant. Unfortunately, its population is also threatened by humans who consider it an important food source and as well as an organ donor for human transplants.

The capybara shows you how to be resourceful. Realize your ability to adapt to your surroundings so that you feel more comfortable. Consider some of the changes you can make to improve your living conditions. Something as simple as rearranging your space and adding a splash of color can make you feel more productive. When you learn to live simply and within your means, you will find that your energy level will significantly improve.

Blue Morpho Butterfly

The blue morpho is an exquisite jungle creature and one of the largest butterflies. Its wingspan is over seven inches long. The blue morpho reflects light on its wings, which causes a visual change in shape when flying. To compensate for the morpho's vivid blue color, the underside of its wings are camouflage to resemble the jungle foliage. It's wings also displays eyespots to deter predators. Humans look to emulate the lustrous feature of the blue morpho's wings through what is known as biomimicry. This replication helps with the iridescence aspects of materials designed to avoid counterfeit. Research into this attribute has also inspired the color displays on many of our electronic devices. The interconnectedness of an organism as fragile as a butterfly is as significant as any other living creature.

The butterfly symbolizes the many changes that will take place throughout your life. All of the challenges you overcome are part of your transformation. As you learn and grow, you move further toward fulfilling your life's purpose. Enjoy the process as much as the manifestation of your goals.

Elephant

The elephant is among the most intelligent of all mammals. Their brains are similar to humans and share similar emotions such as playfulness, aggression, and compassion. Elephants are especially concerned about their calves, which stay with their mothers for almost four years after birth. Elephants are also mournful of the dead. They grieve the bodies of their ancestors, participate in burials, and look over the remains of those long deceased. One of the contributions an elephant makes to life in the jungle lies in its excrement, which provides food for insects, invertebrates, amphibians, and other creatures.

Interestingly enough, the Asian elephant's connectedness lies in their rain-filled footprints, often filled with frog eggs and tadpoles. These deeply grooved imprints provide nutrient-rich stepping stones for these amphibians to make their way to other populations. Unfortunately, these remarkable creatures are considered endangered because of the brutal acts of poachers. These individuals hunt and kill in the primary pursuit of an elephant's ivory tusks.

The elephant spirit invites you to look at the big picture. You come from an ancestral lineage unique to you. Take time to research your family history and listen to the stories of your elders. The more you learn about your relatives, the more you will understand the traits and skills you may have inherited. The process of this exploration is sure to enrich your life and help you define the best version of yourself.

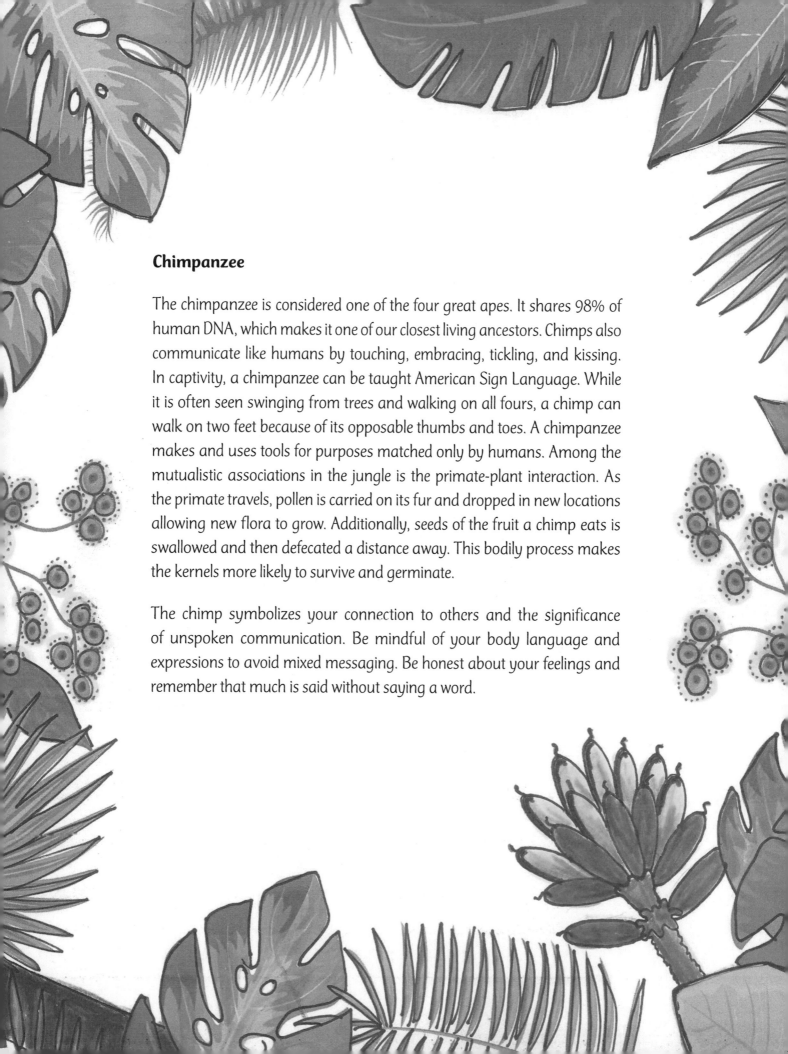

Chimpanzee

The chimpanzee is considered one of the four great apes. It shares 98% of human DNA, which makes it one of our closest living ancestors. Chimps also communicate like humans by touching, embracing, tickling, and kissing. In captivity, a chimpanzee can be taught American Sign Language. While it is often seen swinging from trees and walking on all fours, a chimp can walk on two feet because of its opposable thumbs and toes. A chimpanzee makes and uses tools for purposes matched only by humans. Among the mutualistic associations in the jungle is the primate-plant interaction. As the primate travels, pollen is carried on its fur and dropped in new locations allowing new flora to grow. Additionally, seeds of the fruit a chimp eats is swallowed and then defecated a distance away. This bodily process makes the kernels more likely to survive and germinate.

The chimp symbolizes your connection to others and the significance of unspoken communication. Be mindful of your body language and expressions to avoid mixed messaging. Be honest about your feelings and remember that much is said without saying a word.

Lemur

Easily recognized by its spotted fur and a tail longer than its body, the lemur lives in Madagascar's rainforests. Lemurs spend most of their lives on the ground and within the mid-canopy of trees. Lemurs love to soak in the sun's rays in the morning and enjoy a diet of fruit, leaves, bark, and insects throughout the day. The lemur has been called an unintended gardener of the rainforest. It ingests the seeds of trees and ultimately disperses them on the forest floor. A group of lemurs observed in the wild reveal a playfulness with each other. And, they are rarely skittish around humans.

The message of the lemur is to be brave enough to take on the adventures in your life. It is understandable to feel anxious about new situations. However, you can choose to approach opportunities with strength instead of fear. By lightening up, you will enjoy more of what each occasion brings.

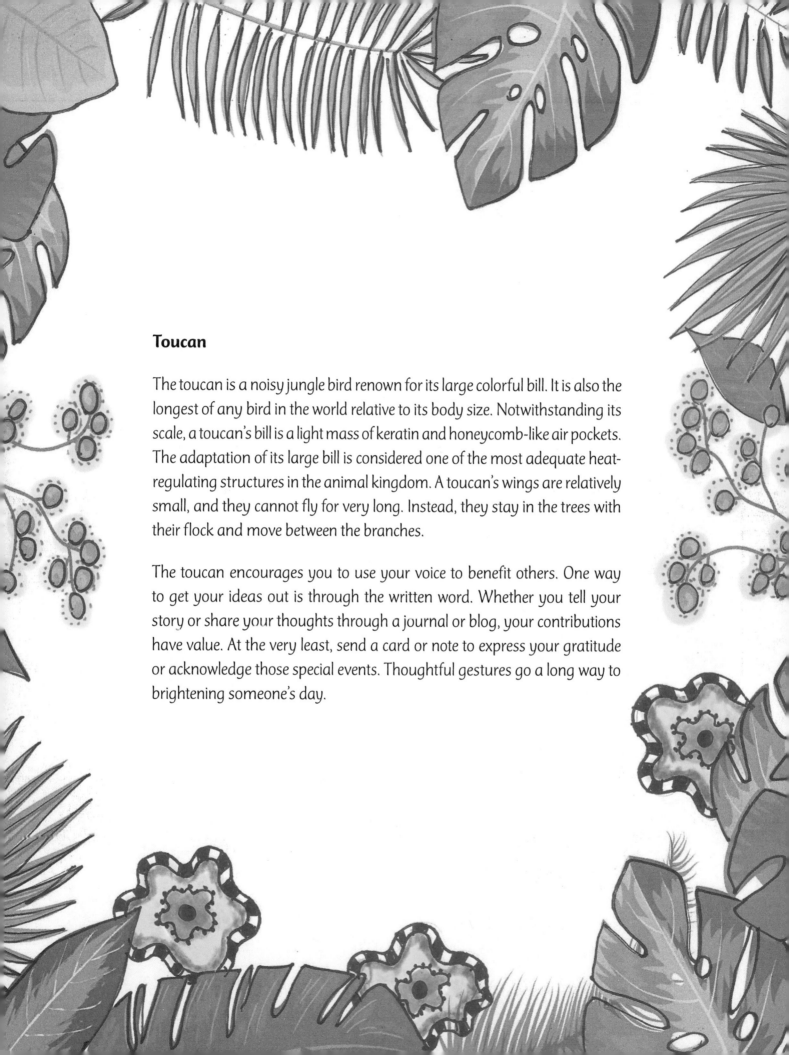

Toucan

The toucan is a noisy jungle bird renown for its large colorful bill. It is also the longest of any bird in the world relative to its body size. Notwithstanding its scale, a toucan's bill is a light mass of keratin and honeycomb-like air pockets. The adaptation of its large bill is considered one of the most adequate heat-regulating structures in the animal kingdom. A toucan's wings are relatively small, and they cannot fly for very long. Instead, they stay in the trees with their flock and move between the branches.

The toucan encourages you to use your voice to benefit others. One way to get your ideas out is through the written word. Whether you tell your story or share your thoughts through a journal or blog, your contributions have value. At the very least, send a card or note to express your gratitude or acknowledge those special events. Thoughtful gestures go a long way to brightening someone's day.

Gorilla

Gorillas are the largest primates in a jungle ~ weighing an average of 400 pounds. They grow to over 5 feet tall. A notable characteristic of this creature is that their arms are longer than their legs. Gorillas are known as knuckle-walkers. Their hands and feet are like a human in that they have opposable thumbs and big toes. Gorillas are mainly herbivores. They eat around fifty pounds of food a day to include leaves, fruit, bamboo, and insects. The gorilla is highly intelligent and can use sign language to communicate with humans. Unfortunately, gorillas are endangered. In addition to being hunted, the Ebola virus has killed enough of the species to have brought them in danger of extinction. Fortunately, ecotourism, which includes guided trips to see gorilla populations, provides a source of income for local people. It also highlights the importance of environmental conservation programs.

The gorilla totem emanates a quiet dignity and invites you to do the same. Whenever you take on a leadership role, there is no need to be boastful. Have confidence in your abilities and maintain your integrity. Knowing your self-worth will add to your charisma. Ultimately, it is also what will earn you respect.

Rainforest Beetles

The diversity of beetles on earth exceeds 360,000 species ~ more than any other creature. Beetles found in the rainforest are the largest on the planet. A beetle, such as a titan, has measured at 7 inches. They help decrease the population of harmful parasites. Simultaneously, their movement aids in the spread of helpful nutrients and seeds that nourish a jungle's ecosystem.

The beetle's message involves evaluating situations in your life that might require you to compromise. Perhaps you are asked to take on a responsibility that is more challenging than you anticipated. Find a way to understand the significance of what you are doing and how it helps a higher good. See the task as a stepping stone that strengthens your emotional skelicature. When your interactions with others depend on your ability to be empathetic, you have the opportunity to develop your character in ways you may not have otherwise experienced.

Jaguar

The jaguar is the world's third-largest cat. Excluding a few feet of the tail, they grow to over 5 feet long and weigh over 250 pounds. Jaguars are sometimes mistaken for leopards. The difference is in their larger head, shorter legs, and the black dots in the middle of their circular markings known as rosettes. Jaguars are undiscriminating hunters in that they eat almost anything. The name jaguar means 'he who kills with one leap' because they slay with the power of their bite. Their teeth strength allows them to chaw through even the thickest hides and shells of other animals. Despite it being illegal, the jaguar is susceptible to poaching. A jaguar's teeth and claws are wanted for jewelry, and their pulverized bone powder is used for medicinal purposes.

The jaguar models physical endurance. It shows you how to conserve your energy so that you will have it when you need it the most. Visualize the direction you want to go in your life, and then persevere. Practice self-care every day. Understand the importance of a healthy diet, exercise, and a good night's sleep. Every action you take to nourish your mind, body, and soul will add to your resilience.

Howler Monkey

The howler monkey is known for its discordant cry that can be heard over three miles away. The males have large throats and vocal chambers that help increase their ruckus volume. In a group, the howler shrieks send the message that the territory is being occupied. This primate has a strong gripping tail, which it uses to hang from branches. It takes full advantage of the jungle lianas as it moves about the trees. Howler monkeys are rarely on the ground. Instead, they stay away from predators and enjoy munching on their leafy diet.

The howler monkey teaches you to rise above your challenges and make the best of situations, no matter how complex. Take the high road when you are tempted to lash out. Restrain yourself no matter how heated the circumstances, and find a peaceful solution.

Chameleon

Over 150 species of chameleons are known to exist ~ ranging in size from a half-inch to a few feet. A chameleon is best known for blending in with its habitat, and that includes a diverse jungle. The outer skin is transparent, followed by layers of pigment that mix or absorb heat to create new skin tones. A chameleon's colors can attract a mate or deter an enemy. Most noticeable is a chameleon's eyes that move in two directions, which give it a panoramic view of its surroundings.

Not surprising, the message of the chameleon is to blend into life's situations as needed. Alter your responses depending on what is happening at the moment. Know when to speak up and when to pull back. Discern when it is best to stay and work things out versus when to walk away. It is possible to meet each scenario in life differently while still staying true to yourself.

Every creature on earth depends on another to survive. This reliance extends to all aspects of an ecosystem and ultimately our planet. Human beings have a tremendous responsibility for supporting the health of the environment and the survival of all that exists. We can feel good about doing our part and showing we care.

Understanding the circle of life helps us recognize our connection with others. As with the animals in a jungle, we can learn to respect the diversity of humankind. Knowing that all lives are precious highlights the unique qualities that each person brings to the world. When we can celebrate our similarities and differences, we'll more fully appreciate how we share the human experience.

For additional jungle facts and meanings,
check out the following resources to learn more:

Rainforest Alliance.org
National Geographic Kids.org
One Kind Planet.org
Life Science.com
Spirit Animal.info
What Is My Spirit Animal.com
Legends of America.com
Rainforest Animals.net

Printed in the United States
by Baker & Taylor Publisher Services